Janet Moss

MACMILLAN TYPING TASK BOOKS

Typing Problems

Paul Bailey

First edition 1979
Reprinted 1981 (twice)

Published by
THE MACMILLAN PRESS LTD
London and Basingstoke
Companies and representatives throughout the world

British Library Cataloguing in Publication Data

Bailey, Paul, b. 1937 (Dec.)
Typing problems. – (Macmillan typing task books).
1. Typewriting
I. Title
652.3'024 Z49

ISBN 0-333-26210-7

Printed in Hong Kong

TYPING TASKS - TYPING PROBLEMS

This book of over 107 exercises provides a wide range of typing problems for students preparing for public elementary and intermediate examinations. It is intended to supplement material found in any basic text and in particular *Comprehensive Typing* and *Typing for Colleges for elementary and intermediate examinations*. It provides practice material for students taught by teachers who prefer not to use a basic text - but teach from their own material. The exercises range from the very simple - they can be used by non-examination students - to the intermediate level.

Although specific instructions are given for the typing of all exercises many have been composed in such a way as to provide additional exercises - typed according to the instructions given and then at the discretion of the teacher. For example the Theory Tests, which begin the book, could be typed just as they are - while the exercises on hanging paragraphs could be typed in the blocked and indented styles to provide yet more practice material. Students can be instructed to type the original exercises again - after they have been corrected by the teacher, using correction signs; the permutations are numerous.

The Contents page shows the range of problems offered. Many of the exercises are in simple manuscript to provide practice in an important area of any public examination and the whole book leads directly to the taking of public examinations.

Two other books complete this present series - *Letters, Postcards and Memoranda* and *Displays and Tabulations*.

The author wishes to thank Margaret Hewines for editing and members of the staff of T P Riley School for providing the handwriting.

CONTENTS

* Linked exercises

Teachers may wish to use this page as an additional exercise - typed as it is or in alphabetical order.

THEORY TEST

Answer the following as indicated by your teacher

1. What size of type face gives:

   (a) 12 letters to every 25 mm (1 inch)
   (b) 10 letters to every 25 mm (1 inch)?

2. How should you take paper out of a typewriter?

3. What is the name given to paper which measures:

   (a) 210 x 148 mm
   (b) 210 x 297 mm
   (c) 148 x 210 mm
   (d) 200 x 250 mm
   (e) 200 x 325 mm?

4. What should you do with your typewriter when you finish using it for the day?

5. What is the platen?

6. Why should you use a backing sheet?

7. How many sheets of paper are there in a ream of typing paper?

8. What is the advantage of using a typing mat? What is the difference between mats used for manual machines as opposed to those used with electric machines?

9. What is an all-black typing ribbon called? What do you call a two-colour typing ribbon?

10. What would you use the following weights of typing paper for?

    (a) 70 g/m^2 (b) 45 g/m^2 (c) 100 g/m^2

THEORY TEST

Answer the following as indicated by your teacher

1. How should you lift a typewriter?

2. What precautions should you take before moving an electric typewriter?

3. What is another name for:

   (a) a 10-pitch machine
   (b) a 12-pitch machine?

4. What is the 'ready-to-type' position?

5. What is a blocked paragraph?
   What is a hanging paragraph?
   What is an indented paragraph?

6. When should you use the ampersand (&)?

7. How should you correct:

   (a) an error using an eraser
   (b) an error, using an eraser, made when taking one or more carbon copies
   (c) an error made when taking one or more carbon copies and using correcting fluid?

8. What is the difference between:

   (a) a shoulder heading and a paragraph heading
   (b) a main heading and a sub-heading?

9. What margins and paper would you use for the following letters using (a) pica type (b) elite type? 100 words 250 words

10. What are side or marginal headings?

THEORY TEST

Answer the following as indicated by your teacher

1. What sizes of envelopes should you use for the following:

   (a) a sheet of A4 paper folded twice horizontally
   (b) a sheet of A4 paper folded to give A6
   (c) a sheet of A4 paper folded once
   (d) a sheet of A5 paper flat
   (e) a sheet of A4 paper flat?

2. What is the correct order for an address?

3. Where should you type the address on an envelope?

4. How should carbon paper be stored?

5. What do the following correction signs mean?

   (a) ⊏ (c) trs (e) # (g) l.c.
   (b) u.c. (d) NP (f) stet (h) /

6. What are superior characters?
   What are inferior characters?

7. How would you produce accents if you had to type a foreign language passage containing them and you did not have them on your machine?

8. How should you type on a wax stencil?

9. How should you clean a typewriter?

10. What is the difference between the ratchet release and the interliner?

Paper: A4
Type this article using a main heading, shoulder headings and paragraph headings.

CENTRAL BUILDING SOCIETY

When you think of saving or investing money, there are several points to take into account. Here we set out some of these points.

SUBSCRIPTION SHARES

Regularity is the top secret of saving money. First you decide how much to save each month - from 50p, one share, in multiples of 50p up to £32.

Interest on regular savings is allowed, basic rate income tax paid by the Society. You can draw out the money and interest at short notice.

PAID-UP SHARES

You can invest amounts from £1.00 to £15 000.00 in paid-up shares.

Interest is paid, tax paid at the basic rate, and you can withdraw your money and interest when you need it. Because the rate of interest is higher than that paid on Subscription Shares the Society may require a month's notice of withdrawal.

DEPOSIT ACCOUNTS

Amounts up to £15000 can be placed in a Deposit account.

Interest is credited half-yearly on 31 March and 30 September. It can be sent to you, paid into your bank account, or added to your account half-yearly on 1 April and 1 October. Tax, at the standard rate, is paid on interest.

Paper: suitable. Type the article using shoulder and paragraph headings. You may wish to indent paragraphs.

BANKING FOR STUDENTS

Especially those about to leave School or College

As a student you will have a fixed amount of money to live on and will need an efficicent means of dealing with you money - and banks can assist.

READY MONEY

A current account enables students to make any payments - providing they have sufficient money in their account - by means of cheques. No interest is paid on current accounts but account holders may use a Cheque Card to prove their ability to pay small sums. An Automatic Cash Dispenser card enables an account holder to withdraw money from a bank - even after closing hours.

OTHER ACCOUNTS

A savings account provides interest on money deposited by means of a pass book - which is also presented when withdrawals are made. Students may draw up to £20 at a time as a rule.

A deposit account is very similar to a savings account but there are no rules as to how much can be put in a deposit account. Students who wish to withdraw money must go to the branch of the bank which keeps their account. Interest is paid as for a savings account.

Paper: suitable. Type the following using shoulder and paragraph headings.

WORLD-WIDE MOTORING HOLIDAYS

Booking Conditions

How to book. A booking can be made through any travel agent, motoring organization or by World-Wide Motoring Holidays. A firm booking will only be made on receipt of a completed reservation together with an appropriate reservation fee.

Confirmation and final payment. On receipt of the reservation form and deposit (or total amount) the chosen holiday will be allocated - subject to availability. A booking confirmation and invoice will then be sent. Any balance due must be paid no later than 8 weeks prior to departure - if not the company reserves the right to cancel the booking and retain the deposit. Tickets will be sent 3 weeks prior to departure.

Cancellations. If after booking and paying the deposit any person wishes to cancel their holiday they must notify the company in writing at once.

Holiday Insurance [We have arranged an exclusive insurance scheme so that all persons travelling with the company may be covered automatically under a Master Policy held by us.

The Premium. Add the premium to your holiday deposit - no proposal form need be completed. Adults £3.00 each children 4-14 £2.00 children under 4 free.

Paper: suitable. Type the lettered section using hanging paragraphs.

VALLEYS

Valleys are an important geological feature and from the evidence of space satellites they may be a feature peculiar to our planet. Three main types can be distinguished.

A Those created by the wearing action of water. These are characterised by a V shape and the more vigorous the action of the river or stream creating the valley, the steeper the sides. Older water created valleys are often very wide.

B Those created by glacial activity where ice and rocks carried in it gouge out valleys. These are characteristically a U shape and are found only in areas which have been subjected to glacial activity. Many glacial valleys also show evidence of the cutting action of a stream - probably caused by the melting glacier.

C Rift valleys are created when the land between two faults slips. Such valleys are very steep sided. The Red Sea is a drowned rift valley.

Paper: suitable. Type the following using hanging paragraphs for the numbered section.

CULTURAL HINTS

Fuchsias are easy to grow and produce masses of flowers for long periods. With proper care and the right environment, some varieties will flower all the year round. The following hints apply to cuttings received through the post.

1. Unpack as quickly as possible and pot in 50 mm pots using John Innes No. 2 compost. Place in a shaded place for 2 or 3 days before exposing the plants to full light.
2. Pot on as soon as the roots show through the bottom of the pot, increasing the size of the pot as required.
3. Start feeding after 4 weeks with a good general liquid fertilizer. Fuchsias are tropical plants and require a good balance of moisture, heat and humidity to produce the best results.
4. To produce plants of good shape, pinch out the growing tip after the third leaf break. Pinch out side growths at the second leaf break. No more than 3 pinchings out should be required.

With care, plants should last for many years and are best propogated by taking cuttings in March each year.

Paper: suitable. Type the lettered sections inside the paragraphs. Repeat typing them outside the paragraphs.

TRENDS IN RETAILING

Figures, published over the past few years, show a marked change in the pattern of retail distribution. The small corner shop is rapidly vanishing as the bigger groups rationalise and concentrate. The most marked changes are:

(a) the multiples (which include such stores as Woolworths and Marks and Spencer) have increased their share of the market to over 41%;

(b) affiliated independent multiples (such groups as APT and Spar) have taken over 18% of the market;

(c) mail order accounts for roughly 5% of the retail market;

(d) the share of the market of the independent retailers has fallen from roughly 50% to under 20%.

Indications are that the trends will continue and that in future the shopper will shop at fewer, if larger, stores than at present.

Paper: suitable. Type the lettered sections inside the paragraphs. Repeat and type them outside the paragraphs.

BUYING A CAR

Some Practical Considerations

For most people buying a car, be it a new one or a second-hand one, represents the second-largest purchase of their life - the largest purchase being a house. The following probably enter the considerations of most people:

(a) How much the new car will cost - taking into account any allowance they might be given on a car they are trading-in in part exchange.

(b) How many passengers the car will carry - it is no use buying a car with five seats when only one person will use it at a time.

(c) How much petrol the car needs to cover a certain distance - running costs are an important consideration.

(d) The cost of spare parts and servicing. All cars go wrong at some time and the availability of spares and servicing Agents are important factors to be considered.

(e) The cost of insurance - some quite small cars demand a high insurance premium.

(f) How fast the car will go and how quickly it will accelerate.

(g) Last - but by no means least - the safety features built into the car.

Paper: suitable. Type the lettered sections: bracketed on one side only - inside the paragraphs; bracketed on one side only - outside the paragraphs.

ELECTRICAL POWER

Electricity is taken for granted today yet a hundred years ago its possibilities could not have been forseen. It plays an important part in the daily lives of all - from communications to cooking. Its most convenient forms are :-

a) that provided by the electricity industry from power stations. The vast part of all electricity consumed is produced in this way and it has the advantage of being available at all times at the flick of a switch. It is also the cheapest form of electricity per unit consumed;

b) that provided by batteries for use in portable equipment. This is a very flexible method of producing and consuming electricity although it is quite expensive;

c) that produced by portable generators. This method is particularly useful when quite large quantities are required away from the main supplies - or when they are cut off.

Paper: suitable. Use Roman numerals for the paragraphs - typed inside or outside.

GENERAL INFORMATION

Freezing meat

Food is suitable for freezing if it is unlikely to be changed by the process of deep-freezing. Generally food which is to be eaten cooked, fried or baked is more suitable for deep freezing than food to be eaten raw.

(i) Use only best quality meat. Any parts damaged or soiled during killing should not be frozen

(ii) To ensure tenderness, meat must be drained before being cut up and frozen.

(iii) All meat should be carefully wrapped before freezing. Meat should be prepared compactly and smoothly so that no protruding pieces damage the packing material. It is advisable to separate pieces with grease-proof paper to prevent them freezing together.

(iv) Length of storage time depends on the quality and composition of the meat or meat products.

Paper: suitable. Use Roman numerals for the paragraphs - typed inside or outside.

CHOOSING WINE

More and more people are drinking wine with their meals - if only on 'special' occasions. There is still a great deal of ~~mystic~~ MYSTIQUE about the choice of wines but some simple comments can make selection much simpler.

17.

xx(i) Choose a wine you like - even if it is not considered to be 'quite right' for the meal. It is pointless wasting money on wine you - or your guests - dislike.

x(ii) If in doubt chose a red wine for a meal with red meat - beef - and a white wine for fish or poultry.

(iii) If the meal consists of both red and white meat - for example when eating out - chose a Rosé wine.

x(iv) French wines with the words Appellation Controlée are generally a safer purchase than those without some other distinguishing information.

xx(v) Buy from a reputable wine merchant or store - their reputation has been earned and they will not want to damage it.

x(vi) Do not be afraid to ask the assistant or wine waiter for advice.

(vii) Keep a record of wines you have enjoyed in the past - and ask for one you know you like.

Paper: suitable. Use Roman numerals for the paragraphs - typed inside or outside.

WIRING INSTRUCTIONS ✓

The wires in this mains lead are coloured in accordance with the following code:-

BLUE: NEUTRAL

BROWN: LIVE

As the colours of the wires in the mains lead of this appliance may not correspond with the markings identifying the terminals in your plug, proceed as follows:

(i) The wire which is coloured BLUE must be connected to the terminal which is marked with the letter N or coloured BLACK.

(ii) The wire which is coloured BROWN must be connected to the terminal which is marked with the letter L or coloured RED.

(iii) Make sure that a 3-amp fuse is used in the mains plug. The correct fuse is coloured BLUE.

If you are in any doubt, consult a qualified electrician.

Paper: suitable. Type the numbers inside the paragraphs. Repeat, typing them outside the paragraphs.

CHOOSING WHERE TO LIVE

While it is probably true to say that many people have little real choice about which part of the country they will live in, family ties and jobs playing a restrictive influence, some choice may be possible in the following areas:

1. The locality in which people choose to live. This may simply revolve about the cost of the property and it may not be a question of what area but what house at a given price in any area.
2. What type of accommodation people require. Single people may be quite happy living in a flat, even a shared one - while families may require a house. Some people will seek the privacy of a detached house while others seek the cheapness of semi-detached property.
3. The nearness, or otherwise, of main-line communications and such facilities as shops, hospitals, schools and places of entertainment.

It probably comes down to what people can afford and personal considerations.

Paper: suitable. Type the numbered paragraphs with the numbers outside - and then repeat with the numbers inside the paragraphs.

SAVING MONEY

Most people find it difficult to save any money but for those who have the will-power to do so the following provide safety and interest for savings – both large and small.

1. The Post Office provides a number of options from The National Savings Bank to the purchase of Government Stock. For the small saver the Post Office has the advantage of long opening hours and many outlets.

2. Commercial banks offer Savings Accounts and Deposit Accounts for those who want interest on their savings. One problem is the opening hours of banks – they are closed when most people are not at work.

3. Building Societies offer a range of savings accounts – all with useful interest which is tax paid at the standard rate. This is particularly important to those who pay income tax. Building societies offer longer and more convenient opening hours than banks.

Paper: suitable. Type the numbers, bracketed on one side only, outside the paragraphs. Repeat, typing them inside the paragraphs.

PAPER

Paper is taken so much for granted by many people yet the choice of paper for any given situation may say a great deal about a person. A caring person will take trouble about the kind of writing/typing paper used and the following types of paper communicate information about the sender as well as information from what is written/typed.

1) Does the paper match the colour/quality of the envelope in which it is sent? Routine communications from an office may be sent in cheap envelopes to save costs but private communications demand greater attention to detail.

2) What is the quality of the paper? A very thin bank paper will not create the impression given by a good-quality bond paper.

3) Colour plays a part in indicating the character of the sender and as a rule it is advisable to use a good-quality white paper to one with exotic tints.

4) Is the paper ruled or plain? A typed letter should not be sent on ruled paper, which if used for handwritten communications might suggest a lack of confidence on the part of the sender.

Paper: suitable. Inset the numbered section.

APPLYING PAINT

It is a pity to waste time and money applying paint without taking some care to ensure a good job.

1. Remove all loose material from the surface to be painted. All surfaces should be clean, dry and free from grease and rust.
2. Apply a coat of rust preventer to cleaned metal surfaces or a coat of primer to bare or unsound surfaces.
3. Apply the top coat of paint evenly and liberally. Too much is as bad as too little – one will cause the paint to 'run' while the other will not cover the surface in a satisfactory manner.
4. Paint on a fine dry day – it is pointless painting outside if it is raining or rain is due before the paint dries.

It is common sense to use a top coat with a compatible undercoat – a light top colour can hardly be expected to cover a dark undercoat in one application.

Paper: suitable. Inset the numbered section.

EXAMINATION HINTS

Most people do not enjoy taking examinations and many do not perform as well as they can because of nerves. While it may not be a bad thing to feel a little apprehensive about an examination the following will help.

1. Make sure that you have revised thoroughly. You cannot hope to do well if you have not revised. If the examination is a practical one make sure you are not out of practice.
2. Arrive at the place of the examination in good time so that you are not rushed or flustered. Ensure that you have the correct equipment with you - and some form of identification should it be required.
3. Spend some time reading through the paper before you start and ensure that you answer the questions set - not the ones you have revised in anticipation regardless of what is asked on the paper.
4. Do not spend all your time on one or two questions to the exclusion of others which might have to be answered.

Above all - try to keep calm.

Paper: suitable. Inset the section numbered with Roman numerals.

LONG-PLAYING RECORDS

Long-playing gramophone records are marvels of modern science and are so common-place that it is easy to lose sight of the fact that they are expensive.

To ensure maximum pleasure and life from long-playing records

(i) Store them upright away from heat. If they are stored flat they tend to warp and buckle.

(ii) Always wipe them clean of any dust before playing - taking care to keep fingers off the playing surface. The use of anti-static fluid helps to keep them dust-free.

(iii) Use a stylus which is in good condition to play records. A worn or damaged stylus will quickly ruin any record.

(iv) Make sure that the playing arm on the record-player is as light as possible - the heavier the weight the greater the wear.

(v) Do not play one record on top of another.

If in any doubt, consult your record dealer for advice.

Paper: suitable.
Type the following, changing the numbers to figures.

The largest lake in England, Lake Windermere, is ten point five miles long, is two hundred feet deep and has a surface area of five point six nine square miles. This is very small when compared to the largest lake in the world - the Caspian Sea. With a total surface area of some one hundred and forty-three thousand five hundred square miles, it is roughly seven hundred and sixty miles long and three thousand two hundred feet deep. The Caspian Sea - or inland lake - is salt water. The largest fresh-water lake in the world is Lake Superior with a total surface area of thirty-one thousand eight hundred square miles but the lake with the largest volume of fresh water - some five thousand seven hundred cubic miles - is Lake Baikal. This lake is also the deepest in the world at an estimated six thousand three hundred and sixty-four feet.

Type the following on a suitable sheet of paper. Change the numbers to figures.

When it is reported that sixty-three students were away from their studies because of illness on a particular day or that nine thousand eight hundred and thirty-five people watched a particular game, it is possible to prove the figures. What is not so easy is to prove such figures as those given in nineteen hundred and fifty-three for the population of Cuba - eight million, five hundred and fifty-three thousand, three hundred and eighty-four - or that given in nineteen hundred and seventy-one for the population of England - forty-four million, eight hundred and seventy thousand and fifty-one. It is fascinating to imagine who could calculate these figures with such accuracy - one wonders at what exact moment the count was made and what account was taken of those being born or dying. It is easy to be exact about the size of a particular sheet of paper and say that A four paper measures two hundred and ten millimetres by two hundred and ninety-seven millimetres. At least you can measure and check for yourself!

Paper: suitable. Change the words to figures as required.

STOCK EXCHANGE REPORT ✓

Blackwood Hodge scored a gain of nine pence to eighty-four pence following a thirty-two per cent jump in profit and a four millions δ seven hundred and fifty thousands pounds surplus. Gold shares fell δ but losses rarely exceeded fifteen pence. Elsewhere mines improved up to sixteen pence. Fisons gained eleven pence at four hundres and δ two pence with General Electric Company firmer at two hundred and eighteen pence - a rise of nine pence. Other leaders five or six pence firmer included Tesco, thirty-nine and a half pence, Beecham at six hundred and twenty three pence and Davy International at two hundred and thirteen pence. Oils were firmer behind Wall Street with British Petrolum up twelve pence at seven hundred and fifty-one. In e a much calmer market, most shares managed a small technical recovery.

Paper: suitable. Type a correct copy of the following.

The balance of Payments caps and underscore

l.c./l.c. The Balance of Payments is the net flow of money into or out of
a a country after taking into account the blance of trade and
#/u.c./a trade in invisibles. the blance of trade is the net flow of
money in to or out of a country after considering trade in and
visible goods such as raw materials, semi-manufactured goods &
manufactured goods. Just as there is trade in visible goods
'/' there is also a trade in what are known as invisibles - services
a trs which result in flow of moeny into and out of a country. run on

stet The services which make up the invisible trade are such ~~things~~ items
① as tourism, banking insurance and the payment for the carriage
of goods in ships and air craft in all parts of the world.

When a country imports more visibles than it exports its trade
trs is siad to be in deficit while if it exports more than it
imports it is said to be in surplus. When more money flows out
l.c. of a country than into it taking both visibles and Invisibles
c into acount its balance of payments is said to be in deficit
trs while if more moeny flows in it is said to be in surplus.

Paper: suitable. Type a correct copy of the following.

The division of labour — Caps

① Increasingly, in modern societies, there is a trend to break
up a complex task into a series of simple, easy ~~jobs~~ tasks. Instead
of one person performing all the oper ations required to produce
a particular article, several people under take just one part of
the whole. run on

stet In this way each person becomes ~~a specialist~~ ~~an~~ expert in one simple
trs |-| task and is so able to perform it very quickly ~~and~~, the whole
s proces of production is speeded up. The simpler the series of
tasks, the more it is likely that machinery will be used and the
NP process speeded up still further. [The disadvantages of the
division of labour are that just performing one task many times
trs over makes it boring and because the fianl product is rarely
seen there is no pride in the work. run on

uc/# Henry ford was one of thefirst to see the many advantages
l.c. to be gained from the division of Labour and he used it to ~~grate~~ great
t advanage in the car industry.

Paper: suitable. Type a correct copy of the following.

ℓ ~~The use of~~ money Spaced caps and underscore

u.c/l.c. All Modern societies use money. Money is a unit of reckoning and
made a medium of exchange. Without money all trade would be ~~maid~~
much more difficult and people and nations would have to resort
a to barter. While barter might be convenient trading way of in
l-l certain situations it is very time consuming the main problem
~~in~~ is deciding how much of this is worth so much of that. The
who other problem is finding a person has what you want and is
prepared to take what you have to offer in exchange.

Caps NP Characteristics of money. To be accepted and used as money any
(?) given object must be portable durable, divisible, malliable and
accepted by all. In addition it must be in scarce supply so
that there is insufficient for all to have unlimited quantities.
NP From very early times metals have been used and while iron is
l-l not durable it rusts away - silver and gold fulfil all the δ
u.c. desired characteristics. It is strange to think that modern
money is not durable at all and is really token money. We use
paper to represent values which ultimately are related to the
l.c. price of Gold even though many people have never owned a gold
coin.

Paper: suitable. Type a correct copy of the following.

The use of tools Caps

ℓ/ℓ One of ~~the~~ several characteristics which distinguish~~es~~ man
\# from the other animals which populate our planet is his ability
⊙/uc to use tools, by using his brain to good advantage, man has
been able to over come both lack of strength and speed to
overcome all other species. An unarmed man would stand little
1-1/1-1 chance other than to try to run away if faced with an angry
bull elephant but a man armed with a modern rifle would have
uc little to fear. he would have even less to fear if he was
driving a tank. run on

run as fast as

While a man could not hope to ~~catch~~ the swiftest animal he would
ed have little difficulty in driving a high power car much faster
NP than any animal could hope to run. [Modern man is developing
stet ~~ever~~ even more powerful and complex machines to assist him in areas
far beyond the expectations of man even a few ago years. trs
is Perhaps the next step to make machines which can think for
themselves and make machines that they consider are required.
Such a thought leads one to ask if it would be possible for
y/# machines to eventuall dominate manhimself.

Paper: suitable. Type a correct copy of the following.

NEW SPEED RECORDS

Improved communications

A glance at recent social history shows that for many speed has
become an obsession. While speed fanatics have concentrated on
how fast cars ships and aero planes can be made to travel a
quiet revolution been going on in the field of communications.
We tend to forget that our ancestors heard of the results of
vital battles which decided the futures of whole nations days
if not weeks after they had happened today we can see events
as they happen in our own homes on television screens. The
humble telephone which is taken so much for granted enables the
sick and lonely to send for assistance or comfort in a way that
is just as important for them as it is for the business man to
contact others at work. No longer must messages be laboriously
written on sheets of paper and given to others to deliver many
thousands of Miles away many days, if not weeks, later. Modern
telecommunications can print messages thousnads of miles away
in the same second as they are entered into a machine.

Type a correct copy of the article on a suitable sheet of paper.

Typist! Use paragraph headings as indicated

Energy – spaced caps

The fight against time caps and underscore

Modern civilisations depend, for ~~there~~ their survival, upon energy which they ~~quantities~~ stet consume in ever increasing ~~qualities~~. |-|
The bulk of energy consumed comes directly or indirectly from what are called fossilised fuels that is from coal or oil. Without energy, life as civilised man knows it would cease.
ONe has only to see what happens in a power cut to realize how true that statement is. l.c. s

Primitive civilisations are not so dependant on modern energy sources and can survive on what ~~is~~ basically animal and human energy sources. The use of modern energy sources can certainly improve the quality, if not the quantity, of life for these civilisations. e are

One alarming aspect for all to consider is that by using new energy sources, (such as atomic power) modern man may make the enviroment so polluted for all - modern and primitive alike - that life as we know it will cease. [The race is ~~both~~ for new energy sources to replace those which are rapidly being exhausted ~~but also~~ for energy forms which do not pollute the planet and are renewable. Two renewable energy sources at present under cosideration are wind and wave power ~~to~~ and it is hoped to use them to produce electricity. n civilisations civilisations NP n

Type a correct copy of the following on a suitable sheet of paper.

Typist! Use paragraph headings where indicated

CAR CARE

~~If you don't you wn't have to!~~ dl

Modern cars are dsigned with the e
problem of corrosion in mind be it from 1-1
the salt used to melt ice on roads in
some countries or the effects of head t
and the abrasion of grit in others.
While many motorists are interested in
keeping their car bright and shiney ~~&~~ and s
spend hours washing and polishing, few
take the rtouble to look underneath. trs

The underside os the weakness of many i
cars and the most damaging corrosion
starts where it cannot be seen. A wise
motoristß keeps a care ful eye on ~~what~~ ~~that~~ which
the passing eye cannot see and takes
care to remidy any problems as they e
arise.

Recent developments suggest that ~~motorists~~ ~~car owners~~ stet
are increasingly aware of rusting and
the consequent loss in value that it
brings. In response to ~~a great deal~~ much stet
of prssure many manufacturers make a e
great deal of their rust proofing H
measures in their advertising literature
In the past it was normal to emphasise
how fast a car would go how the O/#/lc
emphasise is on conservation conservation 1-1
of energy and conservation of the actual
fabric of the car itself. How long one ⊙
wonders will it be before car bodies ⊙
last longer than the working parts ?

Paper: suitable. Type a correct copy of the following using double-line spacing.

Those who have been brought up to learn basic temperatures in terms of so many degrees Centigrade or Fahrenheit would probably be amazed at the problems of those who have to try to convert the scales. The mathematical calculations are not so difficult as the problems of association. Most people know that 32°F is freezing-point and that water boils at 212°F just as they know that it is 0°C and 100°C. Problems tend to arise with such problems as the weather. Is 70°F a warm day? Is a hot oven 320°F or is it 159°C? Once numbers become very large or very small – 1000°F or 500°C, minus 65°F or minus 40°C people are vaguely aware that it is very hot or very cold. Other than that the figures have little real meaning.

Paper: suitable. Type the following in double-line spacing.

The midday weather reports for the world one April morning showed that Tel-Aviv and Malaga were the warmest places at 23°C or 73°F. The coldest place was Helsinki at 3°C or 37°F. The report, of course, did not take account of such places as the North Pole, where the temperature was probably well below 32°F or 0°C or places situated on the equator where temperatures exceed 40°C or 90°F for most of the year. A person who rapidly moved from Beirut, 22°C or 72°F to Zürich 4°C or 39°F on that day would have found the temperature drop of 18°C or 33°F rather chilling. On the other hand a person who rapidly moved from Munich to Athens would have found the rise of 15°C or 27°F from 5°C or 41°F to 20°C or 68°F very warming.

Paper: suitable. Type the following in double-line spacing - typing the abbreviations in full. (Comprehensive Typing page 26).

John began to find th working f a large Co had its advantages
bec he recd a great deal of freedom to work on his own projects.
He was well pd & soon had a good balance in his a/c at t bank.
When he had to go to other firms he was pd exs – provided
he gave the sec a recpt for his claim. After a yr he had
made v good progress & he was given more responsible work
to do togethr w a v good rise. He had to move to a
new dept but this did not worry him bec he knew
th t experience wd be good f him. T experience he
gained togethr w some certs awarded after passg
some exams at t local college shd mean a bright
future f him.

Paper: suitable. Type the following in double-line spacing without abbreviations.

Clive used t bnk services to t full to pay his debts. Cheques wh came w his current a/c were v useful f paying f many odd items wh req more cash than he carried w him. He used his bnk credit card whn his current a/c looked as if it wd be overdrawn if he wrote any more cheques. Any payments made to him were pd into t bnk usg payg in slips wh were issued to him in a book. His regular bills were pd fr his budget a/c wh saved him both time & worry trying to remember to pay t standing orders wh he had authorised to pay his fees t the clubs t wh he belonged.

Paper: suitable. Type the following in double-line spacing without abbreviations.

Elizabeth & Diane decided th it was too wet to play tennis & th they ought to find somethg else to keep them occupied f t afternoon. It was too late to go & see t big film wh was showg at t local town so for a time they had to be content watchg TV. Later Diane was asked to go to t local P.O. for her mother to buy some stamps & post a pkt to the USA. While she was out, Diane decd to 'phone Mark to see if he was still going to t club th eveng in view of t weather.

Paper: suitable.

THE WANDERERS' HOCKEY CLUB
GENERAL COMMITTEE
16 October 19__

The next monthly meeting of the General Committee of the Hockey Club will be held in the lounge of the Club on 24 October at 1930 hrs.

AGENDA

1. Apologies for absence.
2. Minutes of the September meeting.
3. Matters arising from the minutes.
4. Secretary's report.
5. Treasurer's report.
6. Team reports.
7. Report from the entertainments committee.
8. Report from the fund-raising committee.
9. Proposed extension to premises.
10. Insurance.
11. Appointment of a new coach.
12. Any other business.
13. Date and time of next meeting.

Elizabeth Walmo
Hon. Sec.

Paper: suitable.

OLDFIELD SPORTS CLUB

OLDFIELD

17 April 19..

There will be a meeting of the General Committee in the Club House at 1800 hrs on 28 April.

AGENDA

1. Apologies
2. Minutes of the last meeting
3. Matters arising from the minutes
   (a) Estimates for new furniture
   (b) Proposed changes to the club rules
4. Secretary's Report
5. Treasurer's Report
6. Report from athletics section
7. Report from entertainments sub-committee
8. Proposed trip to National Sports Centre
9. Any other business
10. Date, time and place of next meeting

John Beardsmore

Honorary Secretary

Paper: suitable.

CENTRAL COMMUNITY COLLEGE
SOCIAL COMMITTEE

6 July 19--

The first meeting of the newly elected social committee will be held in the Committee Room of the Central Community College on 20 July at 1900 hrs. Please make every effort to attend as this is an important initial meeting.

AGENDA

1. Election of Chairman
2. Election of Minutes Secretary
3. Apologies
4. Minutes of the last meeting
5. Election of sub-committees:-
   (a) Fund raising
   (b) Youth activities
   (c) Adult activities
   (d) Sport
   (e) Old People's affairs
6. Election of Press Officer
7. General Secretary's report
8. Treasurer's report
9. Any other business
10. Date and time of next meeting

Jill Dando
Hon. General Secretary

Paper: A4

Minutes of the Youth Activities Sub-Committee of the Central Community College held in the Committee Room at 1600 hrs on 19 October.

Present:
Mary Bickley
Peter Davidson (Chairman)
Jill Dando (General Secretary)
Olive Galt.
Robert Lewis
Fay Partridge.

1. Apologies	Apologies were received from Anita Parkes and Derek Wilkinson.
2. Minutes	The minutes of the previous meeting were taken as read.
3. Matters arising	Robert Lewis reported that the application by the football team to play in the District League had been accepted. The College had played three games and won two – drawing the other.
4. Table-tennis	Fay Partridge reported that all four teams were doing well and that there were enough players for two more teams.
5. Musical	There was considerable discussion about the next production and Mary Bickley agreed to obtain some further costings.
6. AOB	Olive Galt raised the question of a trip overseas in the summer. Suggestions were invited for the next meeting.
7. Next meeting	It was agreed to hold the next meeting on 16 November, at 1600 hrs.

Chairman

Date

Paper: A4

Report of the Selection Committee of Oldfield Sports Club held in the Club House at 2030 hrs on 2 July 19..

Present

Ann Franklin (Club Captain)
John Hewson
Keith Lloyd (Coach)
Susan Mason
Wendy Patterson
Mark Ryder

1. Apologies — An apology was received from David Swinnerton, Chairman of the Club. In his absence Ann Franklin took the chair.

2. Minutes — The minutes of the last meeting were read and approved as a true record.

3. Selection — Both the men's and women's teams for the league fixture against West Acre were selected and captains asked to post the lists.

4. Training — Keith Lloyd reported that as the holiday season was approaching there were some problems. In general attendance at training sessions was very good and there were some very good youngsters available now that school examinations were over.

5. Next Meeting — The meeting closed at 2200 hrs and it was agreed to meet in the Club House at 1930 hrs on 16 July.

Chairman

Date

Paper: A4 ✓

MINUTES of the FUND-RAISING COMMITTEE of THE WANDERERS' HOCKEY CLUB held at the Club House on 2 November 19..

Present:

Mr R Anderson (chairman)
Mr C Davis (secretary)
Mr D Foster
Mr M Hewison
Mr P Noakes

1. Apologies	Apologies were received from Mr H Oldfield and Mr N Turley
2. Minutes	The minutes of the meeting held on 4 October were taken as read
3. Matters arising	Mr Foster reported that the social held on 27 October had shown a profit in excess of £120. There were still some outstanding bills but even when these had been settled the figure would be over £120. The Chairman thanked Mr Foster for his efforts.
4. Christmas draw	Mr Noakes said that the tickets had been printed and arrangements were made to ensure their sale by club members
5. New Year dance	Mr Hewison reported that tickets were selling well and that all arrangements were in hand.
6. Next meeting	There being no other business the Chairman closed the Meeting at 2030hrs and announced that the next meeting would be on 5 December.

Chairman
Date

Paper: A5 (210 x 148 mm)
Set out correctly.

p	p	p	p
56	2	11	14
20	18	19	5
12	36	41	15
88	**56**	**71**	**34**

Paper: A5 (210 x 148 mm)
Set out correctly.

p	p	p	p
27	5	14	60
15	10	36	4
18	22	9	18
60	**37**	**59**	**82**

Paper: A5 (210 x 148 mm)
Set out correctly.

£	£	£
180	5	37
61	136	2
9	26	149
£250	**£167**	**£188**

Paper: A5 (210 x 148 mm)
Set out correctly.

£	£	£
4	28	160
87	240	37
276	4	9
£367	**£272**	**£206**

Paper: A5 (210 x 148 mm)
Set out correctly.

£	£	£
27·50	144·00	9·46
36·45	54·00	8·63
89·37	26·05	37·00
190·00	38·50	48·55
14·05	19·27	63·27
3·19	62·12	0·05
12·36	18·00	139·99
£ 372·92	£ 361·94	£ 306·95

Paper: A5 (210 x 148 mm)
Set out correctly.

£	£	£
5·50	327·50	27·00
26·72	10·30	58·48
0·50	18·47	127·92
436·00	19·37	271·83
89·05	100·00	47·98
127·38	45·54	136·50
48·97	206·78	1·19
£ 734·12	£ 727·96	£ 398·98

Paper: A5 (210 x 148 mm)
Set out correctly.

£	£	£
1130·00	5·86	2774·00
932·77	25·94	84·91
0·90	192·87	294·36
420·85	1592·77	89·99
5200·00	1399·00	936·42
697·72	41·92	6·72
1274·50	4·00	4770·00
£9656·74	£3262·36	£8949·68

Paper: A5 (210 x 148 mm)
Set out correctly.

£	£	£
45·97	36·00	67·90
381·13	481·90	84·38
593·77	720·05	927·50
627·80	682·70	28·00
781·95	428·00	213·31
284·01	84·00	9·99
£2714·64	£2432·65	£1331·08

Use the Order from Typing for Colleges or Comprehensive Typing - or any suitable form - and fill in the following information.

Order No. 37/28/5 Date 5 May 19..

Goods ordered from: Commercial Office Supplies Ltd, 27 Queen's Street, NOTTINGHAM NG7 2RD

Goods ordered by: Sabre Engineering Co Ltd, 72 Factory Street, BIRMINGHAM B15 2TT

Quantity	Description of Goods	Cat. No.	Price	Total
10	Slimline De Luxe 9mm Tapewriter	479	25.00	250.00
10	International electric stapling machine	843	68.41	684.10
5	Large deep (300x230x100mm) cash box	SB72	12.50	62.50
5	Floor stand (blue)	394	8.74	43.70
2	15-drawer steel cabinet	SC15	63.96	127.92
				£1168.22

Delivery 21 days

Use the Invoice from Typing for Colleges or Comprehensive Typing - or any suitable form - and fill in the following information.

VAT Reg No 77/4374/C Date 22 May 19-- Invoice No 2374

Carrier: Own Van No. of Packets 7

Supplier: Commercial Office Supplies Ltd. 27 Queen's Street, NOTTINGHAM.
NE7 2RD

Customer: Sabre Engineering Co Ltd. 72 Factory Street, BIRMINGHAM
B15 2TT

Quantity	Description of Goods	Price	Total	Grand Total
10	Slimline De Luxe 9mm Tapewriter	25.00	250.00	
10	International electric stapling machine	68.41	684.10	
5	Large deep cash box	12.50	62.50	
5	Floor stand	8.74	43.92	
2	15-drawer steel cabinet	63.96	127.92	
			1168.22	
	Less 30% discount		350.47	
			817.75	
	Plus VAT @ 8%		65.42	£883.17

E & OE

Use the Statement of Account from Typing for Colleges or Comprehensive Typing - or any suitable form - and fill in the following information.

Ref No 261/C Terms Less 2½% Cash monthly a/c Date 1 June 19..

Supplier : Commercial Office Suppliers Ltd. 27 Queen's Street, Nottingham NG7 2RD

Customer: Sabre Engineering Co Ltd. 72 Factory Street, Birmingham B15 2TT

Date	Ref. No.	Item	Debit	Credit	Balance
30 April		Balance b/d			953.61
4 May	984	Goods	650.25		1603.86
7 May		Cheque		929.11	674.75
12 May	1030	Goods	525.00		1199.75
14 May	43	Returns		10.00	1189.75
20 May		Cheque		633.99	555.76
22 May	2374	Goods	883.17		1438.93
30 May		Cheque			930.19

Use the Order from Typing for Colleges or Comprehensive Typing - or any suitable form - and fill in the following information.

On 4 July by Order No 771/A/41 Siat Hewitson International Ltd, 119 Farrington Road, London EC1 3ER, received the following order from Pirshal Export Co of 18 Everest Road, Liverpool L69 3BX

Quantity	Goods	Ref. No.	Price	Total
50	Takewell Executive Polaroid Cameras	4148	22.50	1125.00
10	Frontier Hi-Fi Stereo Cassette Decks	FR6550	76.90	769.00
100	Goodtime 6 digit LCD Electronic Digital Watches	GT727	25.25	2525.00
10	Frontier Music Centres	FR 6750	150.00	1500.00
				5919.00

Delivery required was within 14 days.

Use the Invoice form from Typing for Colleges or Comprehensive Typing - or any suitable Invoice - and fill in the following information.

On 16 July by Invoice No. 237 Pirshal Export Co. 18 Everest Road, Liverpool L69 3BX, received the following goods, in a consignment of 30 packets, from Siat Hewitson International Ltd, 119 Farrington Road, London EC1 3ER. The goods were delivered in Siat Hewitson's own delivery van. The VAT No. was 77/924/AC

Quantity	Goods	Price	Total	Grand Total
50	Takewell Executive Polariod cameras	22.50	1125.00	
10	Frontier HI-FI Stereos	76.90	769.00	
10	Frontier Music Centres	150.00	1500.00	
100	Goodtime Digital Watches	25.25	2525.00	
			5919.00	
	Less 30% discount		1775.70	
			4143.30	
	Plus VAT @ $12\frac{1}{2}$%		517.91	
				£4661.21

E & OE

Use the Statement of Account from Typing for Colleges or Comprehensive Typing - or any suitable form - and fill in the following details.

Terms 5% Cash Monthly a/c   Date 1 August 19..   Ref No 14/141

Customer: Pirshal Export Co, 18 Everest Road, Liverpool, L69 3BX

Supplier: Siat Hewitson International Ltd, 119 Farrington Road, London EC1 3ER

Date	Ref No	Item	Debit	Credit	Balance
30 June		Balance b/d			16500.25
10 July		Cheque		15500.00	1000.25
16 July	237	Goods	4661.21		5661.76
20 July	1041	Returns		50.50	5611.26
27 July	477	Goods	3750.25		9361.51
29 July	1102	Returns		26.50	9335.01
30 July		Cheque		5500.00	3835.01

Use the Order from Typing for Colleges or Comprehensive Typing - or any suitable form - and fill in the following details.

On 12 September, by Order number 7304 Khera Trading Co. 24 High Street, Bristol, BS8 1TH, ordered the following from De Saulles & Son Ltd, 14 Park Lane, Reading, Berkshire RG6 2AH. The delivery required was 28 days.

Quantity	Good	Cat. No.	Price	Total
250	Shetland wool sweaters in assorted sizes and colours.	SW 405	21·75	5437·50
300	Wool blend maxi skirts in assorted sizes and colours.	WB 221	18·50	5550·00
500	Polyester cotton dresses in assorted sizes and colours	PCD 47	15·50	7750·00
1,000 pairs	Stretch tights	ST 41	1·30	1300·00
				£20037·50

Use the Invoice from Typing for Colleges or Comprehensive Typing - or any suitable form - and fill in the following details.

On 10 October by Invoice No 2341 De Saulles & Son Ltd., 14 Park Lane, Reading, Berkshire RG6 2AH, sent the following goods in 25 packets by National Carriers Limited to Khera Trading Co., 24 High Street, Bristol BS8 1TH. The VAT Registration Number was 23/77/4455.

Quantity	Goods	Price	Total	Grand Total
250	Assorted Shetland wool sweaters	21.75	5437.50	
300	Assorted wool blend maxi skirts	18.50	5550.00	
500	Assorted polyester/cotton dresses	15.50	7750.00	
1000 prs.	Stretch tights	1.30	1300.00	
			20037.50	
	Less 40% Trade discount		8015.00	
			12022.50	
	Plus VAT @ 12½%		1502.81	
				£13525.31

E & OE

Use the Statement of Account from Typing for Colleges or Comprehensive Typing - or any suitable form - and fill in the following details.

Supplier: De Saulles & Son Ltd, 14 Park Lane, Reading, Berkshire. RG6 2AH

Customer: Khera Trading Co, 24 High Street, Bristol. BS8 1TH.

Date 2 November 19.. Terms 5% Cash monthly a/c. Ref No 21

DATE	REF No	ITEM	DEBIT	CREDIT	BALANCE
30 SEPT.		BALANCE b/d			35291·50
4 OCT.		CHEQUE		29750·00	5541·50
4 OCT.	1437	GOODS	1197·50		6739·00
10 OCT.	2341	GOODS	13525·31		20264·31
17 OCT.	911	RETURNS		350·40	19913·91
24 OCT.		CHEQUE		11500·00	8413·91

Paper: suitable.

CENTRAL TRADING CO. LTD.
Balance sheet as at 31 March 19..

	£		£
Share capital:			
Ordinary shares @ £1	41 000	Cash	1 500
5% preference shares @ £1	15 000	Debtors	700
5% debentures	10 000	Stock	18 250
		Fixed Assets:	
Reserves	16 500	buildings	55 000
Profit and loss account	7 650	machinery	14 700
	£ 90 150		£ 90 150

Paper: suitable

TRIAL BALANCE
as at 31 March 19..

	£		£
Wages	20 000	Capital	59 260
Premises at cost	25 000	Bank Loan	4 500
Purchases	4 700	Creditors	1 700
Debtors	500	Sales	5 800
Opening stock	1 300		
Rates (including Water)	570		
Gas and Electricity	940		
Sundry Expenses	750		
Plant and Machinery	17 500		
	£71 260		£71 260

Paper: suitable.

Income and Expenditure Account for the year ended 31 March 19--

Income	£	Expenditure	£
Members' subscriptions	1,587.00	Rates	150.00
Profit on socials	256.50	Secretarial expenses	
Donation	25.00	Postage	148.00
Excess of expenditure		Stationery	19.70
over income	47.45	Telephone	48.25
		Cleaning	250.00
		Purchase of new furniture	1,300.00
	£1,915.95		£1,915.95

Paper: A5. Design a Petty Cash receipt for use in an office. The receipt should contain the following information - you may wish to change the order.

Heading - Petty Cash Receipt

Number of items purchased

Nature of purchase

Amount of the purchase

Department in which purchase is to be used.

Who made the purchase

Where the goods were purchased from

Date

Signature of person issuing the receipt

Paper: A5. Design a Stock Requisition voucher. The voucher should contain the following information and you may wish to change the order.

Head the voucher - Stock Requisition Voucher

Date

Goods required - description and number

When the goods are required

Department requiring the goods

Who wants the goods - their name and rank

Space for person making the request to sign the voucher.

Paper: A4

Design a telephone message form to contain the following information. You may wish to change the order.

Date of the call.
Time the call was taken.
Who took the call.
Who made the call. The position of the caller.
The address and telephone number of the caller.
The message.
For whom the message was intended.
The department in which the person called works.

Paper: A4

Design an information sheet on which particulars of staff can be entered under the following headings. You may wish to change the order.

Surname
Christian name(s)
Address
Telephone number
Car registration number
Department in which employed
Education
Qualifications
Courses recently attended
Telephone number of doctor
Name of doctor
Previous experience
Date of birth

Use the telephone message form from Typing for Colleges or Comprehensive Typing - or any suitable form - and record the following.

At 1045 hrs Mrs W Harmsworth of Trident Insurance - telephone 76473 - made a call to Mike Thorrowgood in the transport section. She wanted some information about a claim for accident damage caused by a delivery van last week. Can Mike contact her as soon as he returns? The call was taken by Jan Peters. The call was made today.

At 1415 hrs Julie Simms took a call for Mrs Mavis Cooke in the Accounts Department. She is asked to call Mrs Susan Greenhough in the Buying Department of Messrs Turner & Yates at 3472 - extension 47. Mrs Greenhough says that there appears to be some problem with Invoice No 37/4493 and it might be useful if Mrs Cooke can have a copy of it with her when she makes the call. The call was made this afternoon.

Use the telephone message form from Typing for Colleges or Comprehensive Typing - or any suitable form - and record the following information.

Late this afternoon - at 1740 hrs - Mr Clive Wilson took a call from a Miss Cooper in the Sales Department at Cooper, Cross & Didcot Ltd, telephone number 19919 - extension 14. The call was for Mr George Jones in the Planning Department - who was with the Sales Director at the time. Can he contact Miss Cooper urgently - it is about a delay in supplying some vital equipment for the Hydro Generator.

At 0830 hrs this morning Miss Margaret Hewines found a message on the telephone answering machine from Mr Geoff Baker of The Nelson Manufacturing Company at 01 774 34771. The call was for Mr Douglas Bickley in the Drawing Office. Apparently there are some serious design problems on the propulsion unit for the boat they are developing. Can Mr Bickley contact Mr Baker as soon as he arrives and be ready to go and see him should the need arise? Mr Baker is arranging transport.

Use the information form - produced earlier - or the one from Comprehensive Typing page 113 and record the following information.

William Rogers lives at 23 Sussex Street, Halifax. HX3 OHG - he is not on the telephone. He has 'O' levels in English Language, Mathematics, Physics, Chemistry, Biology and History. He attended The Central School, Bolton, and is at present on day-release.

Alison Mary Padfield lives at 139 Banbury Road, Cheadle Hulme, Cheadle, Cheshire. SK8 6EF

Her telephone number is Cheadle 4144. She has a B.Sc. degree from Liverpool University in Human Biology. Before she went to University she attended the High School at Oldham.

Use the information form produced earlier - or the one from Comprehensive Typing page 113 and record the following information.

Miss Anne Powell lives at 44 Fern Grove, Bletchly, Milton Keynes, MK2 3HQ Telephone Milton Keynes 5701. She was awarded a BA in Social Science after taking an Open University course. She attended The William Brookes School in Shropshire.

Mrs Edna Jarrett lives at 67 Claverley Drive, Exeter, EX1 3EG - telephone Exeter 8015. She has 'A' levels in English Literature, Economics and Geography, a Certificate of Education (Cert. Ed.) and a BA degree in Education - University of Warwick. She attended Bexhill High School.

Type this appointments itinerary on a suitable sheet of paper.

ITINERARY

Mr J Durno - 16 April

0845	*Telephone Head Office for up-to-date information on the Atlas Project.*
0915	*Bayliss & Carpenter, Central House. Mr G Bayliss, Sales Manager.*
1115	*Arckwright & Collins, Industrial Estate. Mr A Childlow, Sales Director.*
1230	*Lodge Hotel. Lunch with Mr A Wells of International Engineering.*
1500	*Institute of Civil Engineering. Mr T King, Head of Research Unit.*

Type this appointments itinerary on a suitable sheet of paper.

ITINERARY

Mrs V Maxwell - 19 July

0930	*Chamber of Commerce, North Parade. Miss B K Grace, Secretary.*
1130	*Afro-Asian Exporting Company, Wharf Lane. Mr R Singh, Company Secretary.*
1345	*Telephone Head Office and speak to Mr Rickardo in Accounts.*
1430	*Civic Hall, Congress Square. Miss V Mottram in the Welfare Department.*
1600	*Openda & Khan Ltd, Tower Street. Mrs O Tragen, Office Supervisor.*

Paper: suitable.
Compose the following itinerary for Mr R Scott. All the appointments are on 7 May.

At 0915 hrs he has to make a call on Mr J O'Brien, who is the Export Manager at Vari International Limited – their office is in The Parade. At 1045 hrs he is due to meet Mrs A Thackery, who is the Company Secretary of Modern Clothing Suppliers – and her office is in West Park. He has to meet Mr P Simpson of Simpson & Westwood Ltd for lunch at the Exhibition Centre at 1300 hrs. Mr Simpson is the Sales Manager of the company. After meeting Mr C Benbow, the Office Supervisor of Adams + Davies Ltd in River Walk at 1515 hrs, he has to call at the office to collect his tickets and documents for his trip to Lagos.

Paper: suitable.
Prepare the itinerary for Mr D Hawthorne on 18 February 19..

At 0930 hrs he is due at the main office of Enterprise Industries on the Industrial Estate for a talk with Mr. J. Wood of the Planning Department. His next appointment is in Alpine Way at the branch office of Guardian Insurance Company Limited where Mr. A. Price of the Claims Department has asked to see him – the notes are in the folder. After the 1045 hrs meeting at Guardian Insurance he is due at the main office of Bradbury & Sommerfield where he has an appointment with Mr. R. Oldfield at 11·30 hrs. He will go to the Civic Centre for lunch with Mr. Oldfield – who is in charge of the Organisation and Methods section at Bradbury & Sommerfield – at 1330 hrs and both will meet the man in charge of the O and M department at Commercial Enterprises Ltd – Mr. J. Walker. Mr Hawthorne's last appointment is at 1645 hrs – with Mr. F. Little the Design Engineer at Casino Engineering in Lion Street.

Type this travel itinerary on a suitable sheet of paper.

WESTERN SWITZERLAND AND LAKE GENEVA

Day	Itinerary
Friday	By coach from London to Dover and thence by steamer to Calais. Drive to Bethune for dinner and overnight stay.
Saturday	Drive through Northern France to Rheims by way of Douai and St. Quentin. Sightseeing in Rheims.
Sunday	Drive along the valley of the River Marne to Langres for lunch. Afternoon drive to Swiss frontier and Lake Geneva. Arrive at Montreux for evening meal and stay of four nights.
Monday to Wednesday	Stay in Montreux. Optional excursions will be announced later, including trips to Geneva and across the frontier into Austria.
Thursday	Return to France through Pontarlier and Dole to Dijon, the former capital of Burgundy, for dinner and overnight stay.
Friday	By autoroute to Paris for sight-seeing and then to Lens for overnight stay.
Saturday	After breakfast leave Lens for Calais and the return to London via Dover.

Type this travel itinerary on a suitable sheet of paper.

EAST AFRICAN LION SAFARI

Day	Activity
1	Leave London Heathrow for charter flight to Nairobi.
2	Arrive Nairobi early morning and depart for Milimani Hotel and overnight stay.
3	Leave Nairobi at 0830 hrs for drive to Lake Mangara and Mangara Hotel.
4	Drive among the wild life in the Lake Mangara area before returning to the hotel.
5	Leave for day drive to Ngorongoro and overnight stay at the Ngorongoro Wildlife Lodge.
6	Day spent in the Serengeti Park. Overnight stay at the Lobo Wildlife Lodge.
7	Day spent sightseeing in Serengeti Park.
8	Early morning departure for Nairobi via the Masai Mava Reserve. Lunch taken at Keekorok. Overnight stay at Milimani Hotel.
9	Early morning departure from Nairobi for Mombasa and Nyali Beach Hotel.
10-15	Time spent at Nyali Beach Hotel – optional tours will be arranged.
16	Depart Mombasa for Nairobi and return flight to London.

Type this travel itinerary on a suitable sheet of paper.

TOUR NO. 871

8-DAY RHINE CRUISE

Day	Activity
1	Depart Luton for Rotterdam. Drive by coach to Arnhem - stop on the way for evening meal. Embark at Arnhem.
2	Leave Arnhem at roughly 0900 hrs for cruise through industrial West Germany to Duisburg. Time for shopping.
3	Depart Duisburg at 1000 hrs for Cologne. Visit the cathedral.
4	Depart Cologne at 0930 hrs for short cruise to Königswinter for optional trip to the Dragon's Rock. Leave Königswinter at 1300 hrs for Koblenz. Stop at Remagen - on the way - for short trip to the Ahr Valley
5	Depart Koblenz at breakfast time for Rüdesheim and optional trip to the vineyards and the Asbach distillery.
6	Depart Rüdesheim at 0930 hrs for St. Goar. Optional trips to be announced later. Time for shopping at St Goar.
7	Depart St. Goar at 1030 hrs for Düsseldorf. Afternoon free for shopping. Farewell party after optional tour.
8	Leave Düsseldorf at 1000 hrs for Arnhem and coach trip to Rotterdam.

Type the specification on a suitable sheet of paper. Retain the abbreviations.

THE ATLANTIC SALOON

SPECIFICATION

BODY:	All-steel with impact-absorbing front and rear crumple zones and safety-cell passenger compartment.
ENGINE:	Four-cylinder in-line with OHV water-cooled 1100-cc-capacity engine transversely mounted. Mechanical fuel pump.
Capacity:	1098 cc.
Bore and Stroke:	70.5 mm x 71 mm.
Compression Ratio:	9.0 to 1. Twin-choke carburettor.
Battery:	12 volt 36 amp hr.
TRANSMISSION:	Four-speed all-synchromesh gear box with floor gear change. Gears: 1st 3.76; 2nd 2.18; 3rd 1.78; Top 1.00; Reverse 3.62.
BRAKES:	Diagonally divided dual-circuit braking system. Front brakes discs. Rear brakes drums.

Type this specification on a suitable sheet of paper. Retain the abbreviations.

EASTERN STAR - SPECIFICATION

ENGINE:	Four-cylinder, five-bearing crankshaft unit with aluminium alloy cylinder head. OHV with single overhead camshaft.
Bore and Stroke:	76.2 mm (3.0 in); 81.26 mm (3.2 in)
Cubic Capacity:	1442 cc; 72 bhp at 5000 rev.
Cooling:	Water-cooled, closed circuit with expansion bottle and electric cooling fan.
TRANSMISSION:	Front-wheel drive. Four-speed gear box with synchromesh on forward gears. Ratios: First 3.201; second 2.005; third 1.375; fourth 1.000. Reverse 3.474.
STEERING:	Rack and pinion. Turning circle 10.4 m (34.1 ft).
BRAKES:	240-mm (9.5-in) diameter disc at front. 228-mm (9-in) diameter drum at rear with automatic adjustment. Hydraulic dual circuit, vacuum servo-assisted.
SUSPENSION:	Front: Independent. Short- and long-arm coil springs and anti-roll bar. Rear: Four-bar link. Variable-rate coil springs and anti-roll bar. Gas-filled telescope shock-absorbers all round.
COACHWORK:	Four/five-seater, five-door vehicle of all-steel unitary construction.
WHEELS:	165 SR × 13 radial ply tyres on 4½-in rims.

Paper: suitable. Set out with marginal headings.

63 NORMAN ROAD - FREEHOLD DETACHED RESIDENCE

ON THE GROUND FLOOR:

Entrance Porch.	Electric light point and raised tiled floor.
Reception Hall	Light oak strip flooring; hot-water radiator; telephone point, light point.
Front Lounge	5.40 x 3.29 m (18'0" x 10'9") having modern tiled fireplace with gas point. Double-panel hot-water radiator. Two light points.
Rear Dining Room	3.00 x 2.70m (10'0" x 9'0") having double-panel hot-water radiator and french door to rear garden.
Breakfast Room/Kitchen	3.52 x 2.78m (11'9" x 9'3") being part-tiled and incorporating stainless steel sink unit with tiled splashback. Gas and electric cooker points. Tiled floor.
Deep Pantry	Fitted with shelving.

An easy tread stairway leads to the first-floor landing from which radiate the following rooms.

Bedroom 1	4.58 x 3.29 (15'3" x 10'9") with hot-water radiator.
Bedroom 2	3.29 x 2.78m (10'9" x 9'3") also with hot-water radiator.
Bedroom 3	3.29 x 2.78m (10'9" x 9'3") with hot-water radiator and built-in wardrobe.
Part-Tiled Bathroom	Panelled bath, pedestal wash basin and Airing cupboard plus electric immersion heater in lagged copper cylinder.
WC	Separate WC with low-level unit.

OUTSIDE

Built-on Birch Garage	7.58 x 2.55m (25'3" x 8'6") having up-and-over door; two light points and additional power points. Rear door to gardens.

VACANT POSSESSION ON COMPLETION

Paper: suitable. Set out the following using side headings.

42 LADBURY ROAD - ACCOMMODATION

GROUND FLOOR

Porch Partially glazed entrance door.

Reception Hall Power point.

Through Lounge 5.70 × 3.00 m (19'0" × 10'0") having feature stone fireplace, two electric night storage heaters and two ceiling light points.

Dining Room 3.37 × 2.85 m (11'3" × 9'6") having night storage heater and fitted meter cupboard.

Kitchen 2.40 × 2.25 m (8'0" × 7'6") with fitted sink unit having tiled splashback and sill, gas and electric points, excellent Storage Cupboard off and Additional Pantry with fitted shelving.

FIRST FLOOR

Three good bedrooms leading from the landing having wrought-iron balustrade.

Bedroom 1 3.90 × 2.94 m (13'0" × 9'10") having night storage heater.

Bedroom 2 3.90 × 2.85 m (13'0" × 9'6") also with night storage heater.

Bedroom 3 2.70 × 2.25 m (9'0" × 7'6") with Airing Cupboard off with fitted electric immersion heater in large lagged copper cylinder.

Half Tiled Bathroom Panelled bath, wash basin and heat-and-light ceiling fitment.

WC Separate and half tiled.

OUTSIDE

Gardens to front and rear with separate side entrance. Ample car-parking space.

Paper: suitable.
Change the times to the 24-hour clock system.

1. 6.30 am
2. 9.45 pm
3. 1.35 am
4. 7.46 pm
5. 8.50 am
6. 11.55 pm
7. 12.05 pm
8. 4.32 pm
9. 5.59 am
10. 12 noon
11. Five past nine in the morning.
12. Quarter to six in the afternoon.
13. Half past two in the morning.
14. One minute past twelve noon.
15. Twenty minutes past nine in the evening.
16. Five minutes to eleven in the morning.
17. Four minutes past ten in the evening.
18. Eight thirty in the morning.
19. Quarter to mid night.
20. Twelve minutes past six in the evening.

Paper: suitable.
Change the times to am or pm as required.

1. 1256 hrs
2. 2345 hrs
3. 0720 hrs
4. 1040 hrs
5. 1645 hrs
6. 0015 hrs
7. 1855 hrs
8. 1322 hrs
9. 1415 hrs
10. 1601 hrs
11. 0550 hrs
12. 1720 hrs
13. 2020 hrs
14. 0100 hrs
15. 1200 hrs
16. 2359 hrs
17. 1545 hrs
18. 0355 hrs
19. 1958 hrs
20. 0445 hrs

Paper: suitable.
Arrange the times into chronological order in one column. Re-type and change the times to the 24-hour clock system.

1.	5.30 pm	11.	2.30 am
2.	8.16 am	12.	7.15 pm
3.	9.10 pm	13.	10.45 pm
4.	1.04 pm	14.	6.50 am
5.	10.45 am	15.	4.45 pm
6.	12 noon	16.	1.30 am
7.	8.48 pm	17.	3.20 am
8.	10.58 am	18.	8.17 pm
9.	12.01 pm	19.	4.46 am
10.	11.59 pm	20.	9.30 am

Paper: suitable.
Arrange the times into chronological order in one column. Re-type, changing to am and pm.

1.	2155 hrs	11.	1632 hrs
2.	1116 hrs	12.	1816 hrs
3.	1423 hrs	13.	0355 hrs
4.	1918 hrs	14.	0959 hrs
5.	0115 hrs	15.	1645 hrs
6.	1342 hrs	16.	2359 hrs
7.	1721 hrs	17.	1715 hrs
8.	0240 hrs	18.	0249 hrs
9.	2218 hrs	19.	1000 hrs
10.	0805 hrs	20.	2230 hrs

Paper: A5 (210 x 148 mm). Type the following in double-line spacing.

TEST ON FRACTIONS

1. $12\frac{7}{12} + 9\frac{19}{36} + 4\frac{1}{6}$
2. $2\frac{7}{9} \times 9\frac{4}{27} \times 18\frac{5}{18}$
3. $4\frac{1}{2} - 2\frac{3}{4} + 8\frac{5}{8}$
4. $7\frac{19}{21} + 14\frac{1}{7} + 8\frac{3}{14}$
5. $3\frac{3}{4} + 8\frac{7}{8} + 9\frac{4}{5}$
6. $16\frac{5}{27} + 14\frac{8}{9} + 1\frac{19}{54}$
7. $4\frac{1}{8} - 2\frac{3}{4} + 5\frac{7}{12}$
8. $6\frac{7}{9} \times 5\frac{19}{36} \times 12\frac{2}{45}$
9. $9\frac{4}{5} \times 7\frac{9}{10} \times 3\frac{3}{20}$
10. $16\frac{1}{2} + 9\frac{3}{4} - 5\frac{11}{12}$

Paper: suitable.

Type the following taking note of the fractions.

HOMEWORK

1. Add $1\frac{7}{8}$ to $14\frac{3}{32}$ and $5\frac{3}{4}$ to $11\frac{19}{20}$.
2. Multiply $7\frac{5}{12}$ by $18\frac{35}{36}$ and deduct $7\frac{1}{4}$.
3. Divide $3\frac{5}{8}$ by $1\frac{13}{16}$ and add $5\frac{3}{4}$.
4. Convert $4\frac{11}{16}$ and $5\frac{7}{9}$ to decimals.
5. What is $4\frac{1}{2}$ times $106\frac{11}{12}$?
6. Add $\frac{17}{19}$ to $\frac{3}{38}$ and $4\frac{2}{7}$ to $15\frac{13}{14}$.
7. Divide $36\frac{1}{2}$ by $1\frac{3}{4}$ and add $7\frac{5}{28}$.
8. Multiply $10\frac{3}{4}$ by $4\frac{1}{2}$ and add $17\frac{7}{12}$.
9. Convert $\frac{7}{9}$, $\frac{5}{11}$, $\frac{14}{15}$ and $\frac{7}{12}$ to decimals.
10. Add $2\frac{1}{2}$ to $10\frac{3}{4}$ and divide by $1\frac{3}{4}$.
11. Find $\frac{3}{4}$ of $96\frac{1}{2}$ and add $3\frac{7}{8}$.
12. What is $14\frac{7}{9}$ multiplied by $3\frac{13}{18}$?
13. Multiply $7\frac{5}{11}$ by $3\frac{7}{22}$ and add $3\frac{20}{33}$.
14. Deduct $5\frac{1}{2}$ from $18\frac{3}{4}$ and $2\frac{7}{9}$ from $5\frac{1}{18}$.
15. Divide 750 by $\frac{3}{4}$ and 2600 by $\frac{3}{5}$.
16. Find $\frac{3}{4}$ of 960 and $\frac{5}{7}$ of 140.
17. Take $15\frac{10}{11}$ from $25\frac{1}{22}$ and $1\frac{1}{13}$ from $1\frac{1}{4}$.
18. Add $2\frac{1}{2}$ to $3\frac{3}{4}$ and $5\frac{1}{3}$ to $6\frac{7}{8}$.
19. Multiply $16\frac{3}{4}$ by $5\frac{7}{8}$ and add $9\frac{1}{2}$.
20. Divide $36\frac{14}{15}$ by $\frac{3}{5}$ and add $16\frac{3}{20}$.

Paper: suitable. Type the following in double-line spacing taking note of the inferior characters.

ANOTHER SHORTHAND

Just as an office worker may use shorthand to save time so may a chemist use another form of shorthand to quickly note quite detailed processes. A simple equation: $S + 0_2 = SO_2$ is a quick way of recording that one atom of sulphur combines with two atoms of oxygen to produce one atom of sulphur dioxide. A more complex equation: $2Na_2H_2SO_3 + H_2S = Na_2SO_3 + H_2SO_3 + 2H + 2S$ shows that sodium bi-sulphite combines with hydrogen sulphide to produce sodium sulphite, sulphurus acid, hydrogen and sulphur. Perhaps only a chemist could 'translate' the following: $H_2SO_4 + H_2CO_2 = CO(H_2OH_2SO_4)$ or $SO_2 + 2NaOH = Na_2SO_3 + H_2O$ and $C6H_{12}O_6 + H_2SO_4 = 6C + H_2SO_46H_20$. Perhaps most people can 'read' $2H_2 + O_2 = 2H_2O$ - the formation of water from hydrogen and oxygen.

Paper: A5 (210 x 148 mm). Note the use of inferior characters. Use double-line spacing.

CHEMISTRY TEST

What do the following equations show?

1. $Zn + H_2SO_4 = ZnSO_4 + H_2$
2. $Mg + H_2O = MgO + H_2$
3. $Ca + H_2O = CaO + H_2$
4. $CuO + H_2 = Cu + H_2O$
5. $2Hg + O_2 = 2HgO$
6. $CO + H_2O = CO_2 + H_2$
7. $2CO + O_2 = 2CO_2$
8. $S + Cu = CuS$
9. $CaCO_3 = CO_2 + CaO$
10. $H_2 + Cl_2 = 2HCl$

COMPLETE

1. $2NaOH + H_2SO_4 =$
2. $2NO + O_2 =$
3. $CuSO_4 + Zn =$
4. $CuSO_4 + Fe =$
5. $CO_2 + 2NaOH =$

Paper: A5 (210 x 148 mm). Type the following in double-line spacing.

Solve the following equations for x :-

1. $2[3(x-3)] = 4$
2. $3[(x+2)-3] = 4-x$
3. $1 = x+2[x-3(x+4)]$
4. $[2(x+2)]^2 = 0$
5. $[5(x-1)(x-2)]-1 = 7$
6. $2[(x-2)^2+3] = 1$
7. $[(x+2)+2]^2 = 0$
8. $5 = x[3(x+2)]$
9. $[2(x-3)]-[3(x+2)] = 4$
10. $(x+2)^2-2[(x+3)+(x-2)] = 1$
11. $[(x+3)+2(x+2)]^2 = 0$
12. $[3(x-3)]^2 = 4$

Paper: A5 (210 x 148 mm). Type the following in double-line spacing.

1. $2[(x+y)^2+3]$

2. $[(a+b)^2]^2$

3. $[2a+2b-3(a-b)]^2$

4. $[(p+q)^2+(p-q)^2]-p^2q^2$

5. $[a+b^2-2(a-b)^2]-[3(a+b)^2]$

6. $3[(a+b)^2-3ab]$

7. $2[(x+y+z)^2-2xyz]$

8. $[u+t-5(u-t)]^2$

9. $2[(g+h)^2-(g-h)^2]$

10. $[(a+b)^2-c^2]+[(a-b)^2+c^2]$

11. $[(y-3)^2+9]-y^2$

12. $[(p-q)^2]^2-[(p+q)^2]^2$

Paper: A5 (210 x 148 mm). Type the following in double-line spacing.

Work out the following completely:-

1. $3(5+2)-[5(7+2)]$
2. $[(5+3)-2]-[3(2+14)]$
3. $[(5+3)^2]^2$
4. $[7-(4+11)^2]-8$
5. $[6^2+7^2-2(6\times7)]^2$
6. $[(3+11)^2-5]\times4$
7. $6[3(2-12)]\div9$
8. $5[8(3\div2)]$
9. $7[6(4+3)-3(6-11)]$
10. $[4(3+6)]-[3(6-2)]$
11. $[5(8+3)]\div4$
12. $[7(6-4)]\div[8(3+11)]$
13. $[4(3+7)^2]-[6(9-4)^2]$
14. $8[3(7+4)^3]$
15. $6[8(3+11)]\times4[11(21-6)]$
16. $8[5-6^2+3(12+36)]$
17. $[12\div4(3+7)]\div12$
18. $[7(8\div3)]\times[6(5\div2)]$
19. $12[5(8\times3)\div4(6-5)]$
20. $7[8(3+4)]\div6[4(8-3)]$

Paper: A5. Set out the poem correctly.

The heron perches on its nest,
Watching from above;
Demanding young allow no rest,
For caring mother-love.

The months go by, the fledglings grow,
Quite soon they learn to fly;
In search of food themselves will go,
How quickly time goes by!

They search for fish, for voles, for frogs,
Their only fear is Man;
They hunt rivers, ponds and bogs,
To find food where they can.

Paper: A5. Set out the poem correctly.

For days the boat had drifted on
Its compass smashed and sea charts gone,
And all the crew had thought as one
That they were lost and all hopes done.

The look-out's call came loud and clear;
The helmsman gave a heartening cheer,
And all the crew were pleased to
hear
That they were safe, that land was
near.

A brilliant sun burst through the cloud,
As through the sea the sharp bow ploughed,
And overhead the seagulls meowled,
As through the sails the fresh wind
howled.

Paper: A5. Set out the poem correctly.

Deep-freeze, Hi-speed, Supersonic days;
Life is very technical in many, many ways.
These days & modern science keep us on our toes-
It's supposed to make life easier - or so the story goes.

Yet were the days gone by so bad?
Were the wages and conditions sad?
Some folks today may still work hard
And still not get a fair reward.

Our world is faster, brighter too,
There's less hard work for us to do.
The bad old days are long since gone,
Today we have more time for fun.

Paper: suitable. Type a correct copy of the article - use a dictionary as required.

Some common spelling errors Caps and underscore

It is a well known fact that many famous people could not spell very well. It is said that the grate William Shakespeare himself spelt his name 13 diffarent ways. It is a brave person who claims that he or she never makes a spelling error. A cynic might say that a poor speller who types can blaim the typewriter.

Many examiners of English are aware that even quite common words are spelt incorrectly by the majority of students. Is Febuary spelt correctly? What about the following: seperate, ocurr, truely, sinsere, accident, Goverment, Parliment and justise?

One of the major problems is that poor spellers do not recognize words which have been spelt incorectly. The solution would seem to be to read as much as possible, (except for articles of this kind), and to keep a record of all words which others have been kind enough to point out to you that you have spelt incorectly. Very often poor spelling is not a question of lack of ability but one of lack of aplication. Whatever the cause, a poor speller is a bad advertisement for a company - be he or she a typist or an executive.

Paper: suitable. Type a correct copy of the following - use a dictionary to help you correct the spelling errors.

THE PROBLEM OF CALCULATING EFFICIENCY

One of the major barganing counters used by workers to justify a pay or wages claim is that of increaced efficiency. While it is farly easy to mesure how much more a particular person produces in a given time it is not so easy to prove how much extre efficient are departments as the Organisation and Methods and, say, the Acounts.

Many workers do not actualy produce any goods. There function is simply to speed up and assist the production which is under taken by others. The numbers of workers actualy engaged in production is quite small compared with the total population of a country yet it would be false to claim that the few were keeping the many. The truth is that efficient production demands planing and other servises - and that it is difficult to plase a measure of eficiency on these particular activites with acuracy.

Perhaps the most scientific and acurate mesurements of efficiency are those aplied to working machinery. Here it is posible to mesure any loss of performance with a high degre of acuracy. The siad truth is that many machines are not very efficient any more than, it is claimed, are sum workers.

Type a correct copy of the following using a dictionary and any suitable sheet of paper.

THAT 'GREEN GRASS'

There is a saying which claims that the grass is always greener on the other side of the fense. The implecation is that things are allways better in another place or at anther thyme. One 'green pasture' sought eagerley by those still at school or college is the won wich lyes beyond the great divide - the day they leave to go to work.

It is only naturel that young people should want to start to work and become independent - it is part of growing up. What many do not realize is that starting to work caries with it many resposibilitis which canot be seen before. One of these is the resposibility of answering for your own actions. While you are still consid-ered too be a junier their is some visible excuse for any possable misconduct. In the world of work there is no such excuse.

Many people who set up their own home or flat soon find that the basic problem of looking after themselfs occupies a large part of there time. As a child, food is placed before a person at regular intervals - or on demand. Once on your own, you have the privilige of doing it for yourself.

How long before the young worker looks back to the 'grass' he, or she, is in at present? There is another old saying - that which says that schol days are the happiest of your live.

Paper: suitable.

EDUCATION

Each country of the world has its own educational system and that system has either evolved from within each particular country in response to some political or social pressure - or been imported from another country. A country may wish to develop an educational system where none exists and finds it more convenient to import a system used elsewhere rather than wait to evolve its own.

Any student wishing to make a detailed study of the educational evolution of England and Wales could spend years reading all the relevant original texts. One book* lists extracts from all documents issued since 1816 and while it is not what might be considered 'light' reading, it does provide an adequate, if brief, insight into the process of evolution.

---

* Educational Documents England & Wales 1816 to the present day. Written by J. Stuart Maclure.

Paper: suitable.

DOES IT MATTER?

The title might equally be 'who wants to know?' One book* which has sold millions of copies devotes itself to recording all kinds of statistics on all kinds of subjects from the tallest human being, the largest parsnip ever grown and the world's largest structures to the universe and space. Any reader may spend many pleasurable hours browsing through its pages, pausing to marvel at the endurance or stupidity of those whose feats are recorded. From the efforts of people from all walks of life who strive to attain instant fame from some odd activity it may well be that provides an unexpected stimulus.

* The Guinness Book of Records

Paper: suitable.

SOME ODD SOUNDS

What do you think is the connection between the terms 'Long metre', 'Half close' and a Serpent? How about the connection between an added sixth, Billy the Kid, Black Bottom and Banner of St. George? Many may well know the answers to both questions - but in case it is thought that one or both are incorrectly written the answer lies in music in general and a dictionary of music* in particular.

Just as in every-day life there is an ever expanding vocabulary with words being invented to describe new inventions - so does the vocabulary of all aspects of specialized activity have to expand. Just as vocabularies expand it is also evident that they contract and 'redundant' equipment and the words used to describe it fall into decline and lack of use.

---

* The Concise Oxford Dictionary of Music.

Paper: suitable. Type the following paying particular attention to the punctuation.

The telephone kept on ringing and Joan decided that she had better
answer it. "Hello," she barked in an angry voice. There was a moment's silence
before a quiet but authoritative voice enquired, "Is that Renton 7660?" "Yes,"
snapped Joan. There was another pause. "Is Mr. Jackson available please?" asked
the voice. "No," replied Joan sternly. "Could you tell me when he will be available
please?" came the question. "No," snapped back Joan, looking at the clock
and thinking about her break. "In which case may I leave a
message for him?" came the calm question. "I suppose so — but
you'll have to wait while I go and find pencil and paper,"
cursed Joan — ever more angry at the thought of further
delay. She slammed the 'phone on to the desk and
stormed round the office exclaiming in a loud voice to her
friend, "Some people must think I've nothing better to do than
run errands — they might have the good manners to
ring when I'm not having my break." When she was finally
ready to take the message the 'phone was dead. Later, she
learned that her rudeness had lost an important order for the
firm — and with it, her job.

Paper: suitable. Type the following paying particular attention to the punctuation.

David knew that he had to cross the busy main road but was afraid of the heavy traffic. After waiting for some minutes, not daring to venture from the pavement he became aware of a lady with a large dog - also waiting to cross. "Please may I cross with you?" he asked - half afraid "I'm new to this town and have to get to my aunty Margaret's." The lady turned and smiled. "Hello, young man" came the reply. "Why hasn't she collected you?" "I'm going to stay with her for a few days - she's not very well and cannot leave the house - I'm supposed to be keeping her company while uncle Jack's at work," blurted out David. "I thought I could find my way from the station to her house - but I'm not used to this traffic." "Hold my hand then," came the reply "off we go." David, the lady and the dog crossed the road without effort. It was not until he had thanked her that David realized that the lady was blind and had been guided across the road by her dog.

Paper: suitable. Type the following paying particular attention to the punctuation.

"Please Miss," asked Gaynor, "can you lend me a pen?" The teacher smiled. "Certainly," she replied — and walked away. Gaynor thought a moment and enquired, "Miss you said y'd lend me a pen — but you didn't give me one. Can you lend me a pen?" "That is true," said her teacher — "You asked if I could lend you a pen — and I can." Again she turned and walked away, smiling as though enjoying a joke. Some time later Gaynor met the same teacher and enquired, "Why didn't you lend me a pen when I asked you earlier? I asked you twice; twice you said you would — but walked away." "Remember earlier in the lesson when I was talking about saying what you mean?" replied the teacher. "You asked if I could lend you a pen. I can — at any time. You did not say when you wanted it. I merely answered your question." "In which case, I will borrow it now, if I may," replied Gaynor.